FLOWER ON A GRAVE

Poems from Ahmed Nadeem Qasimi

FLOWER ON A GRAVE

Poems from Ahmed Nadeem Qasimi

TRANSLATION
DAUD KAMAL

INTRODUCTION
KHALID HASAN

OXFORD
UNIVERSITY PRESS

OXFORD
UNIVERSITY PRESS

Great Clarendon Street, Oxford OX2 6DP

Oxford University Press is a department of the University of Oxford.
It furthers the University's objective of excellence in research, scholarship,
and education by publishing worldwide in

Oxford New York

Auckland Cape Town Dar es Salaam Hong Kong Karachi
Kuala Lumpur Madrid Melbourne Mexico City Nairobi
New Delhi Shanghai Taipei Toronto

with offices in

Argentina Austria Brazil Chile Czech Republic France Greece
Guatemala Hungary Italy Japan Poland Portugal Singapore
South Korea Switzerland Turkey Ukraine Vietnam

ISBN 978-0-19-547497-8

Typeset in Times(for English), Noori Nastaliq (for Urdu)
Printed in Pakistan by
Print Vision, Karachi.
Published by
Ameena Saiyid, Oxford University Press
No. 38, Sector 15, Korangi Industrial Area, PO Box 8214
Karachi-74900, Pakistan.

CONTENTS

فہرست

INTRODUCTION

A few words about Daud Kamal.

Daud Kamal was not only a marvelous poet but an even more marvelous translator. He came to Urdu literature late, but he made up for time lost by his superb rendering of Faiz, Qasimi, Munir Niazi and some of Faraz, who came as did Daud from their beloved Frontier province. It has been said that the translation of a poem is another poem and some have even gone so far as to say that poetry cannot be translated. We should be glad that those who say such things stop right there and do not go on to propose that poetry should not be translated at all. Were that to be so, can we even begin to imagine how much poorer the world would be with the magic of poetry created in one language and culture staying forever confined to that culture?

Faiz, who found in Daud Kamal one whom the spirit, the muse of poetry moved in its deepest sense and whom he considered an English poet of great merit and imagination, once said that in translating him, sometimes Daud had soared away, being a poet himself. When I was working with Daud — we never met but corresponded at long distance, I from Vienna, he from Peshawar — on a collection of Faiz translation, (first published in New Delhi in the 1980s and by Oxford University Press in an enlarged edition here in Pakistan last year) I would sometimes point out to Daud that the rendering was not a precise translation of the original. Daud would respond that what he had rendered was the poem as it had revealed itself to him, as he had felt it. And I think he was right, though I may not have seen his point at the time. If you can capture and transmit the true spirit of a poem or a line of verse and get it right, capture its poetic truth, you have succeeded in doing what is the hardest thing to do in literature: translate poetry into poetry.

Daud began to write poetry while at school — and in English. As I wrote above, he came to Urdu late and for bringing him to Urdu and opening to him the endless variety and richness of Urdu poetry, both classical and modern, we are in Prof. Mazhar Ali Khan's debt, who saw in Daud the genius that was to flower in his own mature work in English and his scintillating translations of poets ranging fromm Ghalib to Munir Niazi. Daud published a number of collections of his English poems, both in poetry magazines abroad and in slim volumes. He won several awards, something that was of the least concern or interest to him. His translations of Faiz that the two of us collaborated on — I dealing with the prose sections dealing with Faiz's life and his views on art, literature and politics — was published after Daud's sudden death in New York where he had come on an exchange programme.

Daud valued Ahmed Nadeem Qasimi highly enough as a poet to have translated so many of his poems. Daud's rendition of Qasimi and the imagery he employs to bring the poem from what is one universe to another is stunning. It may be heretical to suggest this, but Daud's translation of the poem that opens this volume excels the original in its sweep and power. Consider these lines: A new sun will rise one day/I don't know whether from the east /Or the west/From the sky or the bosom of the earth/But a glorious sun/Which will annihilate despair/And will shine forever. Daud's translation of the poem *Dhund* makes one sit up: Deceived by the dawn/A flower awoke/To see all its petals wither/Lost sparrow. Elsewhere, his moonlight coils itself around the poet like a serpent, sharp winds lash his face and palaces of memory and towers of hope stand in the never-ending desert of pain. The blindfolded bull stands 'friendless under the hot sun' making the poet wonder why he does not charge his tormenters. Daud translates Qasimi's night into a figure in a black cloak, with stars in her eyes and dawn on her lips. His recreation of Qasimi's lines about time and change, Daud renders with consummate beauty: Cities are built/Where once were ruins/And songs of joy/Echo in the valley of wolves. Qasimi's satiric summing up of those who dream of revolution but stay grounded in inaction, Daud translates as: The revolution/that fires/the imagination/of my friends/is like/an arrow/that has never/left the bow/a caravan in search of a guide — the print/of/a paralysed/foot.

Saadat Hasan Manto said forewords were unnecessary. He compared them to the little boy who rides in front of the bridegroom to the bride's house. So let me not stand between the poet and his translator, and a fine pair they make in this collection, which, though slim, we can only be grateful for.

Khalid Hasan
Washington

POEMS

The Inner Arctic

Rays
Which were picked up by an exhausted sun
As a crone picks up broken twigs
And half-extinguished embers
Have now returned
Transformed into sparkling snowflakes.
Ice-age inertia—frozen rags of man.
Winds
Which have blown and burned
For centuries
Have been crippled, have collapsed.
The earth's tongue is paralysed.
Eyes stone-blind
Lips blue

منطقہَ داخلی

شعاعیں
جو جاتے ہوُے اِک تھکے ہارے سورج نے
چنگاریوں کی طرح چُن کے دامن میں بھر لی تھیں
اب برف کے نرم گالوں کے فرغل پہن کر پلٹ آئی ہیں
اب دبکتے ہوُے فرش پر پاؤں ٹھٹھرے ہوُے رینگتے ہیں!
ہوائیں
جو لُو بن کے پوری صدی تک چلی اور چلی تھیں
اپاجِ بنی، گر پڑی ہیں!
زمیں کی زباں گنگ ہے
آنکھ پتھرائی ہے
ہونٹ نیلے ہیں

And arms lifeless.
All around
A terrifying wilderness of white
In which our screams turn into an avalanche.

But there is the possibility
Of spring—of life.
A new sun will rise one day—
I don't know whether from the east
Or the west
From the sky or the bosom of the earth—
But a glorious sun
Which will annihilate despair
And will shine forever.

– 4 October 1982

بازو لٹکتے ہُوے، ڈھیلے ڈھیلے ہیں
چاروں طرف اک بھایانک سفیدی کا ویرانہ ہے
جس میں انسان چیخے
تو الفاظ اولوں کی مانند جم جائیں!

اب زندگی کے نکھلنے کا امکان
اِک ایسے سورج سے وابستہ ہے
جو کہیں سے بھی آئے
وہ مشرق سے نکلے کہ مغرب سے ابھرے
وہ افلاک سے گر پڑے
یا زمیں سے نکل آئے ۔۔۔
بس ایک سورج ہو
جو انجمادِ مسلسل کا دشمن ہو
اور ڈوبنا جس کو آتا نہ ہو

جنوری ۱۹۷۷ء

Mist

Mist-enshrouded
The sun rises
Like a disc of tarnished copper.
Static tree-shadows—
Bare branches—
A blighted landscape.
Deceived by the Dawn
A flower awoke
To see all its petals wither.
Lost sparrow. On the road
The loud tap-tap of horses—
Whirling dust.
A balloon-seller

دُھند

کہر میں لپٹا سورج نکلا
دشتِ فلک کے ہاتھ میں جیسے طشت پرانا!
چار طرف اشجار نہیں، اشجار کے سائے استادہ ہیں
شاخیں برگ و ثمر سے خالی
ہریالی بھی دھندلی دھندلی، کالی کالی!
پھول، سحر کے دھوکے میں انگڑائی لے کر پتی پتی بکھر گیا ہے!
چڑیا اپنے رین بسیرے سے نکلی ہے لیکن رستہ بھول گئی ہے!
سڑک پہ تانگے کے گھوڑے کی ٹاپیں گولے چھوڑ رہی ہیں!
ایک غبارے بیچنے والا

In a street empty of children
Doesn't know whether to cry
Or hold his tongue.
Chimney-smoke—dark minaret—dissolves
In the air.
An obstinate child keeps asking his mother repeatedly:
Where is the morning? When will it come?

The mutinous sun has thrown overboard
All the norms of nature. Time walks
On leprous feet. Blotches even on radiant faces.
Leaves fall from the tree of love.

— 3 October 1982

بچوں سے محروم گلی میں آ کر جیسے سوچ رہا ہے
روؤں یا آواز لگاؤں!
چمنی سے جو دھوئیں کا اک مینار اُبھرا تھا
کہر میں جیسے گرا ہوا ہے!
بچہ ماں سے ضد کرتا ہے ۔۔۔ صبح کہاں ہے؟
صبحیں ایسی مَیالی مَیالی کیسے ہوسکتی ہیں!

اک سورج کے دُھندلے پن نے کتنے مسائل جنم دۓ ہیں!
جیسے قدرت کا آئین بدلنے لگا ہے!
وقت بھی جیسے پاؤں گھسٹ کر چلنے لگا ہے!
روشن چہروں پر بھی دھبے پڑنے لگے ہیں!
پتے پیار کے پیڑوں سے بھی جھڑنے لگے ہیں!

نومبر ۱۹۴۸ء

Ghost Town

The moon had blanched
the colours of night.
I walked through a town
where only walls were visible.
Roofs had caved in
Only shadows in the streets.
Bodies were absent.

        – 14 August 1982

خواب

چاندنی نے رنگ شب جب زرد کر ڈالا — تو میں
ایک ایسے شہر سے گزرا — جہاں
صرف دیواریں نمایاں تھیں
چھتیں معدوم تھیں
اور گلیوں میں فقط سائے رواں تھے
جسم غائب تھے!

فروری ۷۶ ۱۹ء

Guide

When night came to the jungle
the eyes of the tiger
blazed into fire-brands of such intensity
that I forgot the sensuous delights
of digressing from the way.

– 14 August 1982

رہنما

رات جنگل میں آئی
تو چیتے کی آنکھوں نے
دو مشعلیں یوں جلائیں
کہ میں راستے سے بھٹکنے کی عیّاشیاں بھول بیٹھا!

فروری ۶ ۱۹۷ء

Ghazal — a fragment

Alone
I must traverse this darkness—
My shadow has fallen on the way
And the wolves of night
Have devoured it.

Moonlight
Coils around me—
Fatal serpent that she is—
And sharp winds
Lash my face.

I have built
Palaces of memory—
Towers of hope—
In this never-ending desert
Of pain.

If you want
To know
How the ship was wrecked,
Ask the drowned sailor—
Ask the murderous sea.

غزل

طے کروں گا یہ اندھیرا میں اکیلا کیسے
میرے ہمراہ چلے گا مرا سایا کیسے

میری آنکھوں کی چکاچوند بتا سکتی ہے
جس کو دیکھا ہی نہ جائے، اسے دیکھا کیسے

چاندنی اس سے لپٹ جائے، ہوائیں چھیڑیں
کوئی رہ سکتا ہے دنیا میں اچھوتا کیسے

میں تو اُس وقت سے ڈرتا ہوں کہ وہ پوچھ نہ لے
یہ اگر ضبط کا آنسو ہے تو ٹپکا کیسے

یاد کے قصر ہیں، امید کی قندیلیں ہیں
میں نے آباد کیے درد کے صحرا کیسے

گر سمندر ہی سے دریاؤں کا رزق آتا ہے
اس کے سینے میں اتر جاتے ہیں دریا کیسے

Outlandish Poetry

My
Verses—
Hieroglyphics
On
The
Walls
Of
Tomorrow—
Language
Of
Blood-Petals
Which
No
One
Understands.

سخن ناشناس

میں جب شعر کہتا ہوں
دیوارِ فردا پہ
میرا قلم
خون کے رنگ میں
پھول سے لفظ لکھتا ہے
لیکن کوئی یہ زباں پڑھنے والا نہیں!

ستمبر ۱۹۷۶ء

Blindfolded Bull

Hide thicker
Than the whip. Does the pain
Never penetrate his bones?
He merely twitches
His ears
Friendless under the hot sun.
Why doesn't he charge
With his black-tipped horns
And rip open
The bellies of his tormentors—
Trample them
Under his torn hooves?
Instead
He flogs himself
With his own tail—
Acolyte in a dark cave—
Sacrificial buffoon.

– 27 May 1983

ایک بیل سے

کھال بہت موٹی ہے تمھاری!
سَن سَن کرتے کوڑے کھاؤ
کان ہلاتے جاؤ!
درد اگر ہڈی میں اُترے
سینگ نہ کام میں لاؤ!
دُم کو گس گس کر خود اپنی پیٹھ پہ مارو
اور نئے کوڑے کی موسیقی سننے کو
سر نیہوڑاؤ!
گھر سے مٹی کھود کھود کر تال ملاؤ!
اور جب ساری کھال اُڑ جائے
صرف ذرا سا ڈکراؤ
پھر چپکے سے مر جاؤ!

اگست ۱۹۷۷ء

Queen of Ebony

Night is not
As cruel
And bloodthirsty
As the tribal elders say.
Nor is she
The shadow of the moon
On a rocky peninsula.
Look!
There she comes—
Carrying a gift for you
Which I am not allowed
To see.
Don't be frightened
By her black cloak.
There are stars
In her eyes—
Dawn on her lips.

– 27 May 1983

طلوع

رات ایسی بھی جابر نہیں ہے
وہ آئی ہے
لیکن تمھارے لیے
کچھ نہ کچھ ساتھ لائی ہے
اس کے سیہ پیرہن پر نہ جاؤ
کہ دامانِ ظلمت میں اس کے
ستارے بھی ہیں
صبحِ نو کے اشارے بھی ہیں

اپریل ۱۹۷۷ء

The Bridled Passion

The clarity
of your body
Surpasses
That of any
Snow-fed stream
And no mountain lake
Can match the serenity
Of your face.
But in your heart
Is the epicentre
Of all earthquakes—
Cauldron
Of leaping flames.

"روح و بدن کے خم و پیچ"

کتنا شفاف ہے بدن تیرا

کل جو تو میرے پاس سے گزری

میں نے دیکھا، کہ تیرے چہرے پر

جھیل کا سا سکون چھایا ہے

اور ترے دل پہ جب نظر ڈالی

میں نے وہ حشر سا بپا دیکھا

جس طرح زلزلہ سا آیا ہے

جون ۱۹۷۶ء

Stone

Don't sculpt in sand, my good artist.
Look for stone.
Only stone makes
A durable work of art.
Red ruby which this callous world
Calls the heart.
Blue sapphire and in it
The eye of betrayal.
Jade of the soul
Streaked with grief's reality.

پتّھر

ریت سے بُت نہ بنا، اے مرے اچّھے فن کار
ایک لمحے کو ٹھہر، میں تجھے پتّھر لادوں
میں ترے سامنے انبار لگادوں—لیکن
کون سے رنگ کا پتّھر ترے کام آئے گا؟

سُرخ پتّھر؟ جسے دل کہتی ہے بے دل دُنیا
یا وہ پتّھرائی ہوئی آنکھ کا نیلا پتّھر
جس میں صدیوں کے تحیّر کے پڑے ہوں ڈورے؟

کیا تجھے روح کے پتّھر کی ضرورت ہوگی؟
جس پہ حق بات بھی پتّھر کی طرح گرتی ہے

White marble complaisant to the touch.
And, then, there is
The legendary diamond of justice too
Which only the rich can buy.

Misbegotten values
Of a misbegotten age.
Grotesque philosophies.
Poetry, dance, music, painting.
My undependable muse.
Your incarcerated intellect.
All are worthless.
All art is trash.
Your hands are stone
And so is my tongue.
Don't sculpt in sand, my good artist.

– 15 June 1983

اک وہ پتّھر ہے، جسے کہتے ہیں تہذیبِ سفید
اس کے مرمر میں سیہ خون جھلک جاتا ہے
ایک انصاف کا پتّھر بھی تو ہوتا ہے، مگر
ہاتھ میں تیشۂ زر ہو تو وہ ہاتھ آتا ہے

جتنے معیار ہیں اِس دَور کے، سب پتّھر ہیں
جتنے افکار ہیں اِس دور کے، سب پتّھر ہیں

شعر بھی، رقص بھی، تصویر و غنا بھی پتّھر
میرا الہام، ترا ذہنِ رسا بھی پتّھر
اس زمانے میں تو ہر فن کا نشاں پتّھر ہے
ہاتھ پتّھر ہیں ترے، میری زباں پتّھر ہے
ریت سے بُت نہ بنا، اے مرے اچھے فن کار

دسمبر ۱۹۶۳ء

Man—The Eternal Enigma

What a strange creature
Is man!
He yearns for that
Which does not exist
But whatever
He is given
He loses no time
In squandering.
Suicidal nihilist
That he is!
He seeks
The imaginary
In the real
And the real
In the imaginary.

– 16 June 1983

آدمی بھی عجیب چیز ہے

آدمی بھی عجیب چیز ہے!
جو نہیں ہے، اسے ڈھونڈتا ہے
مگر جس کو پاتا ہے
اس کو وہ جب تک کہیں کھو نہ دے
کتنا بے چین رہتا ہے!
حاضر کو غائب میں
غائب کو حاضر میں
یوں کھوجتا ہے
کہ جیسے وہ خود کھو گیا ہے!

اپریل ۱۹۷۷ء

Tomorrow

Frozen darkness all around
And no way out.

But man
Sustained by human dignity
Lives on
In the hope
That the first touch
Of dawn
Will melt
This black tundra.

We await
The sun's triumphant return—
The knight
In the golden armour.

– 16 June 1983

وقفہ

راستہ نہیں ملتا
منجمد اندھیرا ہے
پھر بھی باوقار انساں
اس یقیں پہ زندہ ہے
برف کے پگھلنے میں
پو پھٹے کا وقفہ ہے
اس کے بعد سورج کو
کون روک سکتا ہے

دسمبر ۱۹۶۶ء

Resurgence

There is nothing to fear
As long as the creative urge
Is alive.
A bud blossoms
At the very spot
From where the flower fell.
The branch struck by lightning
Is now clad
In the garment of new leaves.
Autumn has never cancelled spring.
This is the essence of life.
Cities are built
Where once were ruins
And songs of joy
Echo in the valley of wolves.

اگر ہے جذبۂ تعمیر زندہ

اگر ہے جذبۂ تعمیر زندہ
تو پھر کس چیز کی ہم میں کمی ہے

جہاں سے پھول ٹوٹا تھا—وہیں سے   کلی سی اک نمایاں ہو رہی ہے
جہاں بجلی گری تھی —اب وہی شاخ   جنئے پتے پہن کر تن گئی ہے

خزاں سے رک سکا کب موسمِ گل
یہی اصل اصولِ زندگی ہے
اگر ہے جذبۂ تعمیر زندہ
تو پھر کس چیز کی ہم میں کمی ہے

کھندر سے کل جہاں بکھرے پڑے تھے   وہیں سے آج ایواں اُٹھ رہے ہیں
جہاں کل زندگی مبہوت سی تھی   وہیں پر آج نغمے گونجتے ہیں

There is nothing to fear
As long as the creative urge
Is alive.
This is the essence of life.
Death's icy hand
Cannot touch you
As long as
Sunbeams quiver on the snow.
Darkness cannot coagulate
As long as
Lamps continue to radiate light.
Man is at war
With his own fate.
This is the essence of life.
There is nothing to fear
As long as the creative urge
Is alive.

– 16 June 1983

یہ سنّاٹے سے لَے کی سمت ہجرت
یہی اصلِ اصولِ زندگی ہے
اگر ہے جذبۂ تعمیر زندہ
تو پھر کس چیز کی ہم میں کمی ہے

نہیں بجُھ بجھنے کا خوف—جب تک شعاریں برف پر لرزاں رہیں گی
اندھیرے جم نہیں پائیں گے—جب تک چراغوں کی لویں رقصاں رہیں گی

بشر کی، اپنی ہی تقدیر سے جنگ یہی
اصلِ اصولِ زندگی ہے
اگر ہے جذبۂ تعمیر زندہ
تو پھر کس چیز کی ہم میں کمی ہے

مارچ ۲ ۱۹۷۲ء

The Evening-Star

When the evening-star appeared
All the flowers
Lifted their heads
From the dark tide
In which
They were submerged.
They looked
At the dazzling star
With profound admiration
And whispered
To one another:
He is one of us.
He is the harbinger
Of celestial spring.

– 17 June 1983

ستارہ شام کا

ستارہ شام کا نکلا

تو پھولوں نے

اُمڈتی تیرگی میں سر اٹھا کر اس کو

دیکھا

اور پھر سرگوشیاں کیں ۔۔۔ :

یہ ہماری نسل سے ہے!

آسماں پر موسمِ گل کا ہراول ہے!

۱۳ دسمبر ۱۹۴۵ء

Village Well

Rope of blood
slithers
from
her hand—
coiled snake
leisurely bathing—
and then
the emergence
of an old
leather bucket
dripping
priceless gems
of
water.

– 17 June 1983

ایک پہاڑی گاؤں کے کنوئیں پر

کنوئیں میں جو رسّی بہی جا رہی تھی
وہ چھلکتی ہوئی اک گلابی ہتھیلی سے نکلی تھی
اور خون کی دھار بن کر بہی جا رہی تھی

پھر اس دھار کو اس گلابی ہتھیلی نے کچھ اس طرح سے سمیٹا
گزوں لمبے اژدر کا اک ڈھیر سا لگ گیا
اُس کے پھن میں لہو تھا

یہ رسّی، بظاہر جو اک ڈول کو کھینچ کر لائی ہے
اصل میں اس چھلی، نرم و نازک، گلابی ہتھیلی کی
صدیوں پرانی مشقت کی سفّاک بے انتہائی کا اظہار ہے

ستمبر ۱۹۷۰ء

The Still-born Revolution

The revolution
that fires
the imagination
of my friends
is like
an arrow
that has never
left the bow—
a caravan
in search of
its guide—
the print
of
a paralysed foot.

– 5 July 1983

جو اِنقلاب

جو اِنقلاب مرے دوستوں کے ذہن میں ہے

وہ تیر ہے، جو کمال چھوڑ کر چلا ہی نہ ہو

یہ کارواں تو عبث رہنما کی کھوج میں ہے

کہ نقش کیسے ملے، جب قدم اُٹھا ہی نہ ہو

Africa

The earth
spins around
a new axis.
Snow falls knee-deep
on the deserts
and the polar regions
are being lashed
by savage sandstorms.
A host
of vanquished suns
stagger and fall
on the western front.
A new day
dawns
from the blazing forehead
of darkest Africa.

– 26 August 1984

افریقہ

دھرتی نے بدل لیا ہے محور
صحراؤں پہ برف گر رہی ہے
قطبین پہ ریت اُڑ رہی ہے
یورپ کے افق پہ ــ لڑکھڑاتی
اک فوج سیاہ سورجوں کی
گر گر کے غروب ہو رہی ہے
شب رنگ جبینِ افرقہ سے
اک صبح طلوع ہو رہی ہے
حبشی نے زمیں کی باگ تھامی
اعزاز بنی سیاہ فامی

دسمبر ۱۹۷۴ء

Remoteness

You are very far
and so is God
but you are not God.
God is beyond space and time.
You I have touched,
embraced, thought, and even understood.
But now you are far
as God is far.

I have seen
the consequences of remoteness.
Thinking that God is remote,
man fragmented Him
into a thousand deities—

دُوری

تو بہت دور ہے
اور دُوری خدا ہے
مگر تو خدا تو نہیں ہے
خدا لمس سے ماوراء ہے
تجھے میں نے چھو کر بھی دیکھا ہے
باہوں میں لے کر سمیٹا بھی ہے
تجھ کو سوچا بھی ہے اور سمجھا بھی ہے
تو فقط دور ہے
تو خدا کی طرح دُور ہے

میں نے دُوری کے اعجاز دیکھے ہیں
انسان نے دور پا کر خدا کو
اسے اَن گنت دیوتاؤں میں بدلا ہے

he carved out their images
and set them up in cold gloomy temples
and worshipped them through desolate centuries.

But you are brimful
with vitality—your blood sings
in your veins—your pores radiate the light
of dawn—your lips are ardent music—
your body is the symmetry of dance.
You are human.
You are colour, poetry, loveliness.
You are life.

It's said
that those who are sundered
are eventually reconciled—
those who go away
come back. But you—
neither God nor deity—
do not return ...
do not return ...

– 2 September 1984

پھر اُن گنت بت بنائے ہیں
اُن کے لبوں پر سکوتِ مسلسل کی مہریں لگائی ہیں
صدیوں کے یخ فرش پر ان بتوں کی قطاریں سجائی ہیں
اور تو دھڑکتی ہوئی زندگی کی حرارت سے لبریز ہے
تیری نس نس میں گاتا لہو دوڑتا ہے
مساموں سے بو پھوٹتی ہے
لبوں پر صدا ہے
بدن رقص کا زاویہ ہے
تو انسان ہے ۔۔ یعنی تو رنگ ہے، شاعری ہے، غنا ہے

سنا ہے کہ انساں اگر دور جاتے ہیں
پھر لوٹ آتے بھی ہیں
تو خدا بھی نہیں
دیوتا بھی نہیں
اور اس پر ستم یہ کہ تو لوٹتا بھی نہیں

جولائی ۱۹۶۷ء

The Burning Taper
a fragment

It's a lie
that death is a void—
a bottomless pit.
I am a river
and my destination
Is the sea.

Life
is a burning taper.
I, too, shall die
but not before
I have ushered in
the dawn.

– 14 September 1984

موت

کون کہتا ہے کہ موت آئی تو مر جاؤں گا
میں تو دریا ہوں سمندر میں اُتر جاؤں گا
زندگی شمع کی مانند جلاتا ہوں ندیم
بجھ تو جاؤں گا مگر صبح تو کر جاؤں گا

اکتوبر ۱۹۶۹ء

Flower on a Grave

Soon after
it stopped raining
I went out
for a stroll
and saw
a wild flower
burst into glory
on a wayside grave
(a suicide's?).
I heard
screams of pain
and hideous laughter
deep down
in the earth.

قبر پہ پھول

اب کے بارش جو ہوئی
میں نے یہ دیکھا
کہ سرِراہ جو اک قبر تھی
(شاید کسی دیوانے کی)
اس پہ اک پھول کھلا ہے
جو ہواؤں کے تھپیڑوں سے تڑپتا ہے
تو پاتال سے ہنسنے کی صدا آتی ہے

جنوری ۶ ۱۹۴۷ء

Writing

The wind writes
on water—the sea
on sand. All artists—
celebrants of life.

A shooting star
scribbles graffiti—
leaves draw circles
in the air.

The spider-web
behind the door
is, in itself,
an astronomer's chart.

Even the dust
is literate—
you'll find its signature
everywhere.

تحریر

ہوا لہروں پہ لکھتی ہے تو پانی ریت پر تحریر کرتا ہے
کہ ہم فرزندِ آدم کی طرح سب نقش گر ہیں
اہلِ فن ہیں
زندگی تخلیق کرتے ہیں
ستارہ ٹوٹ جاتا ہے
مگر بجھنے سے پہلے اپنی اس جگمگ عبارت سے فنا پر خندہ زن ہوتا ہے
— میں مٹ کر بھی آنے والے لمحوں میں درخشاں ہوں —
جو پتہ شاخ سے گرتا ہے
قرطاس ہوا پر، دائروں میں لکھتا آتا ہے
کہ شاخوں پر ٹڑپتے دوستو!
اگلی بہاروں میں مجھے پھر لوٹنا ہے، پھوٹنا ہے، ٹوٹنا ہے، خاک ہونا ہے
مگر وہ خاک، جو اشجار کی ماں ہے
وہ کوندا، جو گھٹا پر ثبت کر کے دستخط اپنے
بظاہر جا چکا ہوتا ہے
چھپ کر دیکھتا ہے
کس طرح تاریکیوں میں زلزلے آتے ہیں
منظر جاگ اُٹھتے ہیں
وہ جالا، جو پسِ درکتنے برسوں سے تنا ہے
اک صحیفہ ہے
کبھی سورج کی کرنوں میں اسے دیکھو
تو پوری کائنات اس میں مجسم پاؤ گے اور جھوم جاؤ گے
کتابیں پڑھنے والے تو نہ مانیں گے
مگر از خاک تا افلاک، جو کچھ بھی ہے، وہ تحریر ہے
الفاظ ہیں، اعراب ہیں، نقطے ہیں، شوشے ہیں، کشیں ہیں، دائرے ہیں، حرف ہیں
جن میں طلسمِ زندگی
اسرار کا اظہار کرتا ہے

Odalisque

The wind tumbles
the clouds—
caresses them
and then transforms them
magically
into a palace
of Arabian Nights splendour.

On the seventh storey
a window
is flung open . . .
an odalisque
(carved out of onyx—
she seems)
sits combing her hair.

عرفان کا حادثہ

ہوا نے بادلوں کو اس طرح تھپکا
کہ وہ جھونکوں کے ہاتھوں میں کھلونے بن گئے
اور آسماں پر اک محل اُبھرا
عجب مرمر تھا اس کا
جس پہ سورج کی شعاعوں کی بنت شہکار فن تھی
صدر دروازہ مقفل تھا
محل کی ساتویں منزل پہ لیکن
اک دریچہ وا نظر آیا
ابھی یہ چوکھٹا تصویر سے محروم تھا
لیکن دریچے سے اُدھر، اک پیکرِ رنگیں کا سایہ سا، ہیولا سا
اک آئینے میں جیسے محوِ آرائش تھا
لمحے ـــ جن کو مستقبل میں آنا تھا

ابھی سے کتنی امیدوں کے گلدستے لیے
سج بن کے بیٹھے تھے دریچے میں

I cannot
take my eyes off her.
Then, suddenly, a cat
pounces on a squirrel.
I look again
but the sun is too hot . . .
everything has melted—vapourized.

                    – 28 October 1984

میں اپنی سانس روکے، آئینے کی اور دریچے کی مسافت میں بھٹکتا تھا
وہ لمحہ جو گزرنے کے لیے آیا تھا
نمیری ٹکٹکی سے ہل نہ سکتا تھا

سرِ دیوار اک بلی، گلہری پر جو چھپی
میں نے دیکھا—— اور فقط پل بھر کو دیکھا
پھر پلٹ کر آسماں پر جب نظر ڈالی
تو مرمر کا محل ٹوٹا پڑا تھا
اور ہوا نے، وادریچے سے گزر کر، اس کی دیمک خوردہ دیواروں پہ
ماتم کے لیے اُٹھی ہوئی انگلی سے
میرا نام
تیرا نام
سب کا نام لکھا تھا

دسمبر ۱۹۷۴ء

Green Cliffs

Those who cry out against oppression
Will be shackled and chained—
Their screams stifled.
But far worse
Is the fate of those
Who run the gauntlet
Of contemptuous eyes.
In the mirror of art
I discovered
That all beauty
Is the creation of man.
The cliff-faces
At the edge of the sea
Are fragrant with greenery
Proving that even stones live.

غزل

مجرم جو صدا کا تھا، وہ زنجیر بپا ہے
اور خانۂ زنجیر کا سرمایہ، صدا ہے*

بستی سے گزرنا اسے دشوار ہوا ہے
ہر شخص فقط ایک طرف دیکھ رہا ہے

دیکھا ہے جب آئینۂ فن میں، تو کھلا ہے
ہر حسن کو انسان نے تخلیق کیا ہے

ساحل کی چٹانوں کے اگر سبز ہیں چہرے
پتھر میں بھی اک سلسلۂ نشو و نما ہے

---

* متاعِ خانۂ زنجیر، جز صدا معلوم—غالبؔ

And as for those who are
Terrified by the wolves of night
There is always hope—
The spear of dawn.
Smash the looking-glass of vanity
And you will see
That you are no different
From other men.
Why plague your mind
With what is good
And what is bad.
Only one thing
Is worth investigating
And that is
The pattern of life.
Interpretations may vary
But the text is the same.
I, too, have seen
The writing on the wall.
In the middle of this wasteland
Grows the tree of my ego
Withered outside but green within.
Why should I submit to your tyranny.
Is not my God the same as your's.

گھبرایا ہوں جب بھی میں گرانباری شب سے
مشرق سے تجلی کا دریچہ سا کھلا ہے

نکلا ہوں میں جب جھانک کے آئینہ جاں میں
جس شخص کو دیکھا، مجھے اپنا سا لگا ہے

انسان کو انسان سمجھنا بھی تو سیکھو
اچھا ہے سو اچھا ہے، برا ہے سو برا ہے

مفہوم میں کچھ فرق ہے، الفاظ وہی ہیں
دیوار پہ لکھا ہوا میں نے بھی پڑھا ہے

یہ عین بیاباں میں شجر میری انا کا
باہر سے اگر خشک ہے، اندر سے ہرا ہے

گر جبر کرے کوئی تو میں جبر سہوں کیوں
جو اس کا خدا ہے، وہی میرا بھی خدا ہے

I live to confirm
The authenticity of love.
I endure
Because truth never dies.
All my life
I have pursued Time.
Perhaps one day
I will catch up with him
And ask:
What is my destiny?

– 31 October 1982

زندہ ہوں کہ شاید اُسے احساسِ وفا ہو
صد شکر کہ ثبت مرا آئینِ وفا ہے

اک عمر سے میں تیرے تعاقب میں رواں ہوں
اے وقت! رے کیسہءَ تقدیر میں کیا ہے

ستمبر ۱۹۷۷ء

Introduction

The whirlwind
which has just passed this way
has been passing
for countless years
every day
exactly at this moment
in the same direction.

Yesterday
when I went forward
to meet it
it brushed me aside
saying:
I am Time
and I do not stop for anyone.

تعارف

ابھی جو ایک ہیولیٰ یہاں سے گزرا تھا
وہ کتنے سال سے
ہر روز
عین اُدس لمحے
یہیں سے — ٹھیک اسی موڑ سے گزرتا ہے!
میں کل برائے تعارف جب اس کی سمت گیا
تو وہ یہ کہتا ہوا میرے پاس سے گزرا
ہے وقت نام مرا
اور گزرنا کام مرا!

جولائی ۷۷۱۹ء

Errata

p. 9	line 3: instead of	مبنار	read	مینار
p. 9	line 8: instead of	بلدنے	read	بدلنے
p. 33	line 4: instead of	جنئے	read	نئے
p. 33	line 9: instead of	کھندر	read	کھنڈر
p. 33	line 10: instead of	ویں	read	وہیں
p. 35	line 5: instead of	شعاریں	read	شعاعیں
p. 35	line 7: instead of	جنگ یہی	read	جنگ
p. 35	line 8: instead of	اصلِ	read	یہی اصلِ
p. 41	line 2: instead of	کمال	read	کماں
p. 43	line 7: instead of	افرقہ	read	افریقہ
p. 45	line 4: instead of	ماوراء	read	ماورا
p. 53	line 5: instead of	ٹوت	read	ٹوٹ
p. 53	line 11: instead of	پوٹنا	read	پھوٹنا
p. 53	line 16: instead of	مین	read	میں
p. 55	line 5: instead of	شعاوں	read	شعاعوں
p. 57	line 3: instead of	نمیری	read	میری
p. 63	line 4: instead of	رے	read	ترے
p. 65	line 4: instead of	ادس	read	اس